CAREERS INSIDE THE WORLD OF

Sports and Entertainment

There are many ways to become involved in the worlds of sports and entertainment. Carlton Eleye is a percussionist for the "Young Nation Band" in Virginia.

CAREERS & OPPORTUNITIES

CAREERS INSIDE THE WORLD OF

Sports and Entertainment

by Bruce McGlothlin

GLOBE FEARON EDUCATIONAL PUBLISHER
A Division of Simon & Schuster
Upper Saddle River, New Jersey

Published in 1995 by The Rosen Publishing Group, Inc.
29 East 21st Street, New York, NY 10010

First Edition
Copyright © 1995 by The Rosen Publishing Group, Inc.

Library of Congress Cataloging-in-Publication Data

McGlothlin, Bruce.
    Careers inside the world of sports and entertainment / by Bruce
McGlothlin.—1st ed.
        p.   cm. — (Careers & opportunities)
    Includes bibliographical references and index.
    ISBN 0-835-91346-5
    1. Sports—Vocational guidance—United States—Juvenile
literature. 2. Performing arts— Vocational guidance—United
States—Juvenile literature. [1. Sports—Vocational guidance. 2.
Performing arts—Vocational guidance. 3. Vocational guidance. 4.
Occupations.]   I. Title. II. Title: Sports and entertainment. III.
Series.
GV583.M344   1995
796'.02373—dc20   95-19047
                                                            CIP
                                                            AC
Manufactured in the United States of America.

Contents

INTRODUCTION

*W*ayne loves football. For several years he has shown outstanding talent as a fullback on the high school team. Many adults and friends have commented on how good a player he is.

He often dreams about the attention and money he could make as a professional football player. This has become his career goal.

But Wayne has a problem: he has let all this go to his head. He thinks all he has to do at school is be a star football player. He thinks that everything should center around him.

As a result, Wayne is doing badly in school. Since reading bores him, he studies very little. His only friends are younger kids who follow him for his athletic skills. Most of Wayne's peers think that he considers himself better than anyone else.

His desire for a career in professional sports has not begun on a very positive note.

Trudy is talented and popular. As a freshman in high school, she became involved with the drama *department. First she was a back-stage helper, then she had parts in several plays. She thinks it is important to experience different roles, both on stage and off.*

Trudy also takes drama and singing lessons to improve her skills. She attends many plays to observe the techniques of others. Discussing her career goals with others in the field has provided her with some good advice.

Trudy also works hard to make good grades, which could mean a college scholarship.

Trudy realizes that to achieve her goal, she must work long and hard. But she also understands that there is no guarantee of success.

Both Wayne and Trudy want careers in the fields of sports and entertainment, but they are moving in different directions.

Trudy's efforts are directed at improving her knowledge and skills in her field. Wayne thinks that playing good football is the only key to success.

Will Wayne and Trudy achieve their career goals? It is difficult to say. But Trudy is working to improve the odds in her favor. Wayne believes he can make it on only pure talent.

If you are interested in a career in either sports or entertainment, let's see what you can do to improve your chances of entering one of these exciting fields.

Michael Jordan, now retired, is considered by many the best basketball player in the history of the game. His success was due to both talent and hard work.

CHAPTER 1

COMMON CHARACTERISTICS

People who want to pursue careers in either the sports or entertainment field have many common attitudes and characteristics.

They possess a high sense of excitement about what they do. Performing in front of an audience encourages them to do their best. It excites them to share their talents and skills with others.

This excitement leads to a real sense of satisfaction about doing what they enjoy most. It is not work; it is play and fun. Often performers become lost in their work. They could do it all day and never become tired.

They are dedicated to hard work to improve their performance levels. They are not afraid to put in long hours to perfect their talents. Increased rewards and positive notice are often the result.

Stevie Wonder is the nickname of the world-famous songwriter and singer Steveland Morris. Right from the start, Stevie had a challenge—he was born blind. His large family lived in a poor section of Detroit, raised by his mother. But Stevie never let his disability interfere with his strong desire to learn and lead a normal life. He loved music. At the age of three, he began his musical career by marching around his home banging pots and pans. His love for music inspired him to learn to play the harmonica, snare drums, bongos, and piano. He often sat for hours on street corners singing and playing his instruments.

By the age of ten, Stevie's reputation had spread. Friends and neighbors appreciated his talents. Soon he was discovered by a member of The Miracles, a nationally known recording group, who introduced him to the president of Motown Records. The rest is history. Stevie has composed, sung, and played many songs that have become best-selling hits. Perhaps his most famous song is "Fingertips, Part I & II." His music continues to bring joy to people throughout the world.

Most people in these fields are highly competitive. They strive to be the best, and they enjoy competing against others. Their self-confidence is high. If they are not the best, that very fact often motivates them to work even harder. They enjoy positive attention. It gives great satisfaction to be appreciated for their skills and talents.

Stevie Wonder has overcome many challenges to achieve his dream of becoming a singer.

For people in the sports and entertainment fields, expectations are high. They must always produce at high levels. They are always under pressure to perform perfectly. Many performers love pressure and thrive on it. They also possess a strong desire to work toward goals that may take months or even years to achieve. Motivation is always high. Nothing must get in the way of reaching their goal.

Professionals in these fields might be described as unique, or "one in a million." Career opportunities are limited because so few openings exist. Competition is intense. While these people must work hard toward their goals, luck and chance always enter the picture.

Beyond these general characteristics, professionals need to possess many specific talents. Top-level performers must have the talent or physical skill to achieve success. The opinions of others may indicate exactly how much talent they do have . . . Do they stand out from others? And by how much?

Upon recognizing that their talent exists, they must have the continuous motivation to develop and improve it. Perfection is the goal. All efforts are focused in that direction.

There are often peaks and valleys in their work. They must acquire the perseverance or staying power to work through the low periods. Many people tend to question themselves during such times. Professionals never lose confidence or lose sight of their goals.

This requires having patience with themselves and with others who may question their talents. They take it one day at a time, always believing in their ability to perform successfully.

The ability to market or sell their talents and skills is also needed. The "right people" have to appreciate what they can do.

Joe Montana was a four-time Super Bowl quarterback for the San Francisco 49ers. He now plays for the Kansas City Chiefs. During high school, Joe was an excellent athlete in football, basketball, and baseball. He was unsure which sport to pursue. Friends and scouts tried to encourage him toward college basketball, but Joe loved football. He believed he was a first-rate quarterback. His goal was to play in the National Football League.

To meet his goal, Joe worked hard to get a football scholarship to Notre Dame. When he arrived, he found other talented quarterbacks who offered stiff competition. So he had to prove himself. During his last two years of college, he began to show his outstanding running and passing skills. Joe became an All-American in football and was drafted by the 49ers. He then went on to stardom as an All-Pro quarterback with many Super Bowl and NFL passing records.

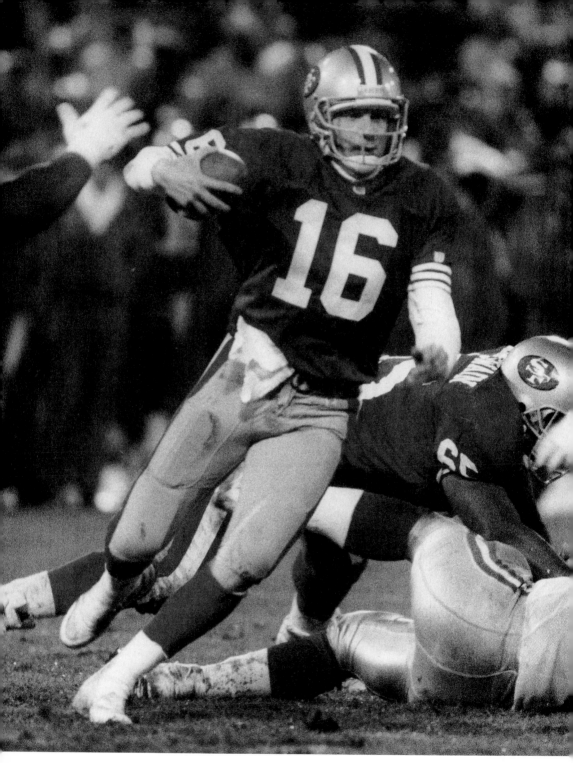

Joe Montana worked hard to reach his goal of playing for the NFL.

Interpersonal skills are valuable in learning to impress others. Relationships are especially important when trying to market skills. If a person is friendly and has excellent talent, the chances of positive contacts improve.

Self-discipline is a common trait in both the sports and entertainment fields. These people are very independent and always seem to know what to do next. They handle both the positive and negative elements of situations. They never lose sight of their goals.

Finally, they possess common sense. They are always aware of themselves and the direction in which they are headed. Flexibility is part of their makeup. They can always redirect their career goals if necessary. Decisions are based on what they think will help them achieve their goals.

Questions to Ask Yourself

Careers in sports and entertainment are very difficult to pursue and require a great deal of dedication and persistence. It's important for you to consider whether you are the type of person suited to such a career. 1) What skills do you need to become successful in the world of sports and entertainment? 2) Do you have the talents and drive necessary for a career in sports or entertainment? 3) What area of sports or entertainment would you be interested in working in?

CHAPTER 2

SPORTS CAREERS

If you enjoy being "in the middle of the action," the following information about "on-the-field" sports careers may interest you.

Professional Athlete

Description: A professional athlete participates in professional athletic events such as football, basketball, and hockey to entertain audiences.

Education: Each sport has its own training and educational requirements. A college education is important because of the higher competition levels and wider public notice.

Talent/Experience: A professional athlete must have speed that is well above average, skill, strength, agility, endurance, and coordination, as well as the ability to perform well under pressure.

Advantages: As a professional athlete, you
16 have the opportunity to participate in the sport

you love. You have a good amount of free time, great health and fitness, and excellent pay.

Disadvantages: The career of a professional athlete is usually short. It consists of constant travel, the threat of injury, the stress of continually playing under pressure, and lack of freedom.

Salary: The salary can run from $100,000 to $5 million per year, depending on the sport and your ability.

Outlook: Positions are limited because of stiff competition.

Tips/Advice: Beginning at a young age, participate in sports. Play at sports camps, and take lessons from coaches. Get involved in outside coaching and playing. Interview athletes in the pro or semipro ranks.

Professional Manager/Coach/Assistant Coach

Description: A professional manager, coach, and assistant coach teach athletes strategies and techniques to prepare for competition.

Education: There are no specific requirements, but many people in these fields have college degrees. Most managers, coaches, and assistant coaches are former college or professional players.

Talent/Experience: You must possess a solid knowledge and love of the sport. You must also have leadership and teaching skills, playing experience, the ability to work well under stress, and excellent communication skills.

Advantages: The excitement of being involved with the sport is a tremendous advantage. You have a good amount of free time during the year. You are able to travel, and you receive good pay.

Disadvantages: Life on the road can be tedious and tiring. There is little job security and you may have to move often. And there is the constant pressure to win.

Salary: The salary ranges from $50,000 to $500,000 per year, depending on the sport, your experience, and your success.

Outlook: Opportunities in the professional ranks may be limited.

Tips/Advice: Become involved in coaching children. Work your way up through high school and college levels. Take coursework around sports training and education.

Professional Umpires and Referees

Description: A professional umpire or referee observes the actions of players to make sure rules of the game are followed.

Education: There are no specific educational requirements. Some people attend special schools for umpires or referees.

Talent/Experience: You must possess a complete understanding of a sport and its rules. You

The life of a professional coach can be stressful, but it can also be extremely rewarding. Former Dallas Cowboys head coach Jimmy Johnson worries before Superbowl XXVII, and celebrates after his team's victory over the Buffalo Bills.

must also have good judgment, good eyesight, and the ability to make quick, accurate decisions. Many umpires and referees are former players.

Advantages: You are able to participate in the sport. You are also able to travel, maintain your health and fitness levels, and receive good pay.

Disadvantages: Life on the road can be tedious and tiring. You must work evenings, holidays, and weekends. It may take a long time to work your way up to professional levels.

Salary: The salary ranges from $40,000 to

Athletic trainers help athletes stay healthy and physically fit. This trainer is helping an athlete stretch out.

$85,000 per year in baseball and hockey, and $500 to $1,000 per game plus expenses in football.

Outlook: The outlook is limited because of the small number of openings.

Tips/Advice: Begin officiating at summer camps or sports events for children. Interview amateur or professional umpires or referees to gain inside tips.

Athletic Trainers and Sports Medicine Personnel

Description: People in these fields help athletes stay healthy, advise teams and players on avoiding injuries, and develop exercise programs and diets.

Education: College degrees in physical education, physical therapy, athletic training, sports medicine, or related fields are necessary for careers in these fields. All trainers are encouraged by the National Athletic Trainers Association to earn a national certificate by passing the written examination and having two years' experience.

Talent/Experience: You must have knowledge of physical education and treatment methods, a willingness to work long hours, and mental and physical stamina.

Advantages: There is much satisfaction in helping athletes avoid injuries and learn better conditioning methods. You have free time during the off season and receive good pay.

Disadvantages: Traveling can be a hassle, and you must deal with long, irregular hours.

Salary: The salary ranges from $25,000 to $50,000 per year in professional ranks and less in others.

Outlook: The outlook is very good for those with the best education and training. Opportunities in the pros may be limited. Other levels are improving.

Tips/Advice: Work as a student trainer for elementary, high school, amateur sports team, or athletic summer camp. Take special courses in sports medicine. Attend college to gain a bachelor's degree or better.

Perhaps you don't think you have the talent or drive for "on-the-field" careers. There are also many "off-the-field" careers that get you closer to the sport you enjoy. Think about these careers, listed according to training required.

On-the-Job Training or Technical School Training

Equipment Managers buy, maintain, clean, and repair all uniforms, equipment, and other materials used in sporting events. Salaries are $20,000 to $30,000 per year. Openings are few.

Groundskeepers prepare and maintain playing surfaces for professional sports teams. Salaries are $15,000 to $30,000 per year. Outlook is good because of the growing number of sports teams at the professional and minor league levels.

Radio/Television Technicians help in broadcasting games. Salaries are $15,000 to $40,000 per year. Outlook is good because of the national expansion of sports radio and television.

Security Guards maintain law and order of crowds at sporting events. Salaries are minimum wage. The outlook is good.

Sporting Goods Store Managers/Clerks sell sporting goods, clothing, and equipment. Managers receive $15,000 to $25,000 per year; clerks begin at minimum wage. Outlook is good.

Stadium Maintenance Workers maintain

Tampa Bay Lightning goaltender Manon Rheaume is the first woman to play in one of the four major pro sports leagues.

the physical condition of the stadium or arena. They include carpenters, electricians, and cleaners. Salaries are an hourly wage, based on a union scale. Outlook is good.

Ticket Salespeople sell or distribute tickets to sporting events by mail or in person. Salaries are $12,000 to $20,000 per year. Hourly positions are also available. Outlook is good.

Ushers help the audience in locating seats and **23**

Paramedics provide emergency medical treatment for athletes during games.

provide other assistance. Salaries are minimum wage. Outlook is good.

Vendors sell food, drinks, and souvenirs during athletic events. Salaries are usually minimum wage, but may also include a percentage of sales. Outlook is good.

Some College or Specialized Training

Amateur Sports Instructors/Coaches teach young people the necessary skills to perform in sports. Jobs pay a seasonal salary or are volunteer positions. Outlook is good.

Bookkeepers keep records and accounts of financial transactions of professional sports teams. Salaries are $15,000 to $25,000 per year. Outlook is good.

Paramedics provide emergency medical treatment and assist trainers and doctors for athletes injured in contests. Salaries are $15,000 to $20,000 per year. Outlook is good.

Photographers take still and motion pictures of athletic contests for professional teams and newspapers. Salaries are $20,000 to $35,000 per year. Outlook is good, but competition is stiff.

Professional Scouts judge athletic skills of college and high school athletes to determine potential for professional sports. Salaries are $20,000 to $50,000 per year. Outlook is good.

Sports Writers/Journalists write newspaper stories about teams and players. Salaries are $18,000 to $50,000, depending on experience. Outlook is good.

Statisticians collect and organize statistical information around sports events, players, and teams. They usually work with radio and television broadcasters. Salaries are $18,000 to $25,000 per year. Outlook is good.

Traveling Secretary makes all travel, housing, and food arrangements for professional sports teams on the road. Salaries are $25,000 to $35,000 per year. Outlook is good.

College Degree or Beyond

Accountants direct and coordinate financial activities of professional sports teams. Salaries are $30,000 to $75,000 per year. Outlook is good.

Announcers/Broadcasters describe sporting events for radio and television audiences. Salaries are $40,000 to $100,000 per year, depending on experience. Outlook is good.

General Managers are responsible for the day-to-day business of the sports team. Salaries are $90,000 to $200,000 per year. Outlook is good.

High School/College Athletic Directors organize and administer school athletic programs. Salaries are $25,000 to $75,000 per year. Outlook is fair.

A cameraman films an Olympic tennis match in Seoul, Korea.

Suzyn Walden is a successful sportscaster who broadcasts the New York Yankees and Knicks games on the city's radio sports channel WFAN.

Owners are the ultimate financial and business supervisors of sports teams. Team owners are usually multimillionaires who have made their money in other industries.

Sports Attorneys perform legal tasks for both teams and players such as arranging leases for stadiums and negotiating contracts for players. Salaries are $75,000 to $150,000 per year, depending on experience. Outlook is good, but competition is stiff.

Sports Doctors provide for general medical care and health of athletes on a sports team. Salaries are paid for specific services and con-

28

sultation provided. Outlook is good, but competition is stiff.

Sports Information/Public Relations Directors promote the favorable image of a sports team to newspapers, radio, television, and the general public. They provide information about teams' goals, accomplishments, and future players. Salaries are $22,000 to $50,000 per year. Outlook is good.

Team Presidents supervise the total operation of a professional sports team and are ultimately responsible to the owner. Salaries are $100,000 to $200,000 per year. Outlook is limited.

Questions to Ask Yourself

Jobs in sports can be very hard to come by, if you set your sights on only playing the game. However, if you keep an open mind and think of other ways to be involved in sports besides being an athlete, you have a much better chance of finding a very rewarding career in sports. 1) Besides professional athlete, what kinds of jobs are available in the field of sports? 2) What types of jobs require education beyond high school? What types of education do these jobs require? 3) What types of jobs might you begin getting experience for in high school?

CHAPTER 3

ENTERTAINMENT CAREERS

If the thrill of bright lights, makeup, costumes, and "on-stage/on-air" performances excites you, here are some careers you may want to consider.

Actors/Comedians

Description: People in these fields entertain and communicate with people by playing dramatic or comedic roles.

Education: No formal education is required, but dramatic training through high school and college may prove helpful.

Talent/Experience: You must have creative ability, poise, patience, the ability to follow directions, and a good speaking voice.

Advantages: You are able to use your creative ability. You receive public attention.

Disadvantages: You work long hours. You

30 don't work regularly. Beginners must work other

Comedians Billy Crystal, Whoopi Goldberg, and Robin Williams are each successful in their own right. They are also the founders of "Comic Relief," an annual show to benefit the homeless.

jobs to support themselves since the pay may be very low.

Salary: Generally governed by union contracts, the average beginning salary is $12,000. Famous movie, television, and stage performers receive $1 to $5 million per year or per performance.

Outlook: The outlook is better than average. Growth is expected, especially in overseas productions.

Tips/Advice: Build on local opportunities in high school, college, and your community. Take acting classes. Work in summer stock (summer theater). Take advice from others in the field.

Dancers perform ideas, using rhythm and sound with their bodies. There are many kinds of dance. The dancers above are members of the Bill T. Jones Arme Zane Dance Company.

Dancers

Description: As a dancer, you perform ideas, stories, rhythms, and sound with your body. Types of dancing include classical ballet, modern, musical, folk, ethnic, tap, and jazz.

Education: There are no specific educational requirements; however, private dance lessons from an early age may be helpful.

Talent/Experience: You must have patience, perseverance, good health, stamina, flexibility, agility, rhythm, coordination, and the ability to work with others.

Advantages: You have the ability to use creative expression and the opportunity to perform. You also receive positive attention from others.

Disadvantages: You must work long hours, including weekends and holidays. The demands of the job are stressful. You must work other jobs to support yourself.

Salary: Generally governed by union contracts, the average salary is $555 to $1,000 per week.

Outlook: The outlook is much better than average, especially in larger cities.

Tips/Advice: Begin serious dance training at an early age. Attend college for further instruction and opportunities. Attempt to join a national dance company for the best job opportunities.

Disc Jockey

Description: People in this field play taped or recorded music on radio or at parties or special occasions. They announce the time, weather, and news. They interview people and make public-service announcements.

Education: No formal education is required, but college or specialized broadcast schools may prove helpful.

Talent/Experience: You must be outgoing, friendly, work well under pressure, relate well to others, and have a good speaking voice.

Advantages: As a disc jockey, you have the opportunity to entertain and become well known.

As a disc jockey, you perform a number of tasks.

Disadvantages: You work alone. You work irregular hours, and there is much competition for the job.

Salary: The average salary is $12,000 to $50,000 per year, depending on experience.

Outlook: There is stiff competition for these jobs. The best chances are at smaller radio stations in rural areas.

Tips/Advice: Build on experience by seeking internships or volunteer positions at college and community radio stations.

The musical group U2 preparing for a concert tour of their album "Rattle and Hum."

Musicians and Singers

Description: Musicians and singers play instruments, sing, write music, or conduct instrumental/vocal performances in public.

Education: No formal education is required, but early training and college-level instruction may be helpful.

Talent/Experience: You must have creativity, poise, patience, perseverance, stage presence, and the ability to perform with others.

Advantages: You can receive enjoyment from performing before an audience and from positive 35

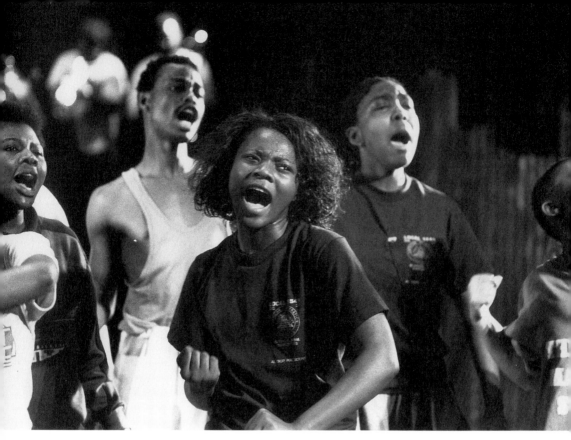

Performances often require a combination of talents. *Township Fever*, the sequel to the South African musical *Sarafina*, stars Zulu singer and dancer Futhi Mhlongo.

attention from others. You display your creative ability.

Disadvantages: The competition is stiff. You must work other jobs to support yourself. Your talent carries no guarantee of success.

Salary: Through union contracts, salaries may range from $22,000 to $68,000 per year. Regional orchestras pay less. Much depends on your professional reputation.

Outlook: The outlook is expected to improve slowly because of stiff competition.

Tips/Advice: Seek opportunities to perform at clubs, restaurants, weddings, etc. Play or perform with name bands. Be able to play several musical instruments. Consider using an agent to get bookings.

If you feel more comfortable "behind the scenes," the following career possibilities can provide a great deal of happiness and satisfaction in the entertainment world. They are listed according to training required.

On-the-Job Training or Technical School Training

Instrument Repairers work to repair musical instruments. Salaries are $21,000 to $26,000 per year. Outlook is good.

Makeup Artists apply cosmetics to face or other body parts for performers. Salaries are $15,000 to $20,000 per year. Outlook is fair.

Piano Technicians identify and correct problems in operating mechanisms of the piano. Salaries are $13,000 to $35,000 per year. Outlook is fair.

Property Managers secure and maintain all stage materials needed for a production. Salaries usually begin at minimum wage. The outlook is limited.

Record Store Managers/Clerks sell records, cassettes, CDs, and audio equipment to the public.

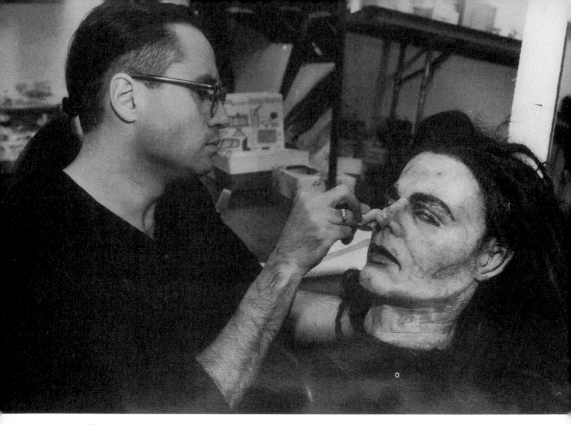

Makeup artist Dennis Bergevin applies makeup to the stage prop of John the Baptist's head. The head is designed to look like the singer who portrays John the Baptist in the opera *Salome*.

Salaries are $15,000 to $30,000 for managers; clerks begin at minimum wage. Outlook is good.

Sound Recording Technicians operate disc and tape recording equipment. Salaries are $15,000 to $30,000 per year. Outlook is fair.

Stage Technicians install lights, sound equipment, and scenery for stages. Salaries are $20,000 to $30,000 per year. Outlook is good.

Studio Technicians monitor the quality of recordings made during production of radio and television programs. Salaries are $22,000 to $32,000 per year. Outlook is good.

Ticket Salespeople sell or distribute tickets

Kerry Cornerford, technical director of the play *Mackerel*, coaxes a one-ton replica of the object of the play through its entry scene. It is the responsibility of stage technicians to set up the stage props and scenery.

to stage and television performances by mail or in person. Salaries are $11,000 to $21,000 per year. Outlook is good.

Ushers assist audiences in finding seats. Salaries begin at minimum wage. Outlook is good.

Video Technicians/Camerapersons work cameras or video-tape machines used to communicate or record performances. Salaries are $22,000 to $60,000 per year. Outlook is good.   **39**

Some College or Specialized Training

Bookkeepers keep financial records and accounts. Salaries are $15,000 to $20,000 per year. Outlook is good.

Choreographers create routines for dancers to perform. Salaries vary tremendously, depending on reputation. Outlook is fair.

Composers write music for singers and musicians. Salaries are usually on commission. Outlook is limited.

Concert Hall Managers supervise all activities relating to the hall or theater. Salaries vary and are based on union rates. Outlook is fair.

Costume Designers design and produce costumes for shows and productions. Salaries are $17,000 to $40,000 per year. Outlook is expected to improve.

Dance Teachers teach dance skills to others. Salaries are usually minimum wage. Outlook is good.

Entertainment Reporters keep the public informed through newspaper columns of shows and productions in the community. Salaries are $23,000 to $45,000 per year. Outlook is good, especially in the smaller market area.

Hair Stylists/Cosmetologists make certain that performers are attractive and well groomed. Salaries are $12,000 to $24,000 per year. Outlook is fair.

Playwrights write plays to be produced on

stage or television or in movies. Salaries are $17,000 to $100,000, depending on experience and reputation. Outlook is good.

Promotion/Marketing Workers promote shows and productions to the community. Salaries are $23,000 to $45,000 per year. Outlook is good, especially in smaller markets.

Road Production Managers plan, organize, and direct all activities of a touring play or show, such as housing, promotion, advertising, and food and beverages. Salaries vary, depending on union scale. Outlook is limited.

Set Designers design and produce sets or background for shows and productions. Salaries are $17,000 to $50,000 per year. Outlook is expected to improve.

Stage Managers coordinate all backstage activities. Salaries are based on union scale. Outlook is good and expected to improve.

Theatrical Agents represent entertainers to schedule them for clubs, concerts, or theatrical productions. Salaries are usually a basic fee or a percentage of the money made at the show. Outlook is fair.

College Degree or Beyond

Accountants supervise all financial affairs of the show. Salaries are $25,000 to $50,000 per year. Outlook is expected to improve faster than average.

Contract Attorneys negotiate contracts for performers on television, radio, and stage. Salaries are $35,000 to $125,000 per year. Outlook is good.

Directors plan, audition, and coordinate their knowledge to achieve the best possible performance. Salaries are $27,000 to $120,000 per year, depending on experience and reputation. Outlook is expected to improve.

Music Teachers teach individuals or groups in schools. Salaries are $20,000 to $30,000 per year. Outlook is fair.

Producers arrange the overall planning, personnel, and production of a show. Salary is usually a percentage of the show's earnings. Outlook is expected to improve.

Public Relations Directors promote and advertise plays or shows to the community. Salaries are $21,000 to $50,000 per year. Outlook is expected to improve.

Questions to Ask Yourself

There are many different fields in the entertainment industry, all of which hold different advantages and disadvantages. You'll have to decide which is the right one for you. 1) If you are considering a career in entertainment, would you prefer to work "on-stage" or "behind the scenes"? Why? 2) What kinds of activities might you become involved in now that might help you in gaining a career in entertainment later?

CHAPTER 4

GETTING JOBS IN THE SPORTS AND ENTERTAINMENT FIELDS

You have decided on a career in one of these exciting fields. Your talents suggest that you would be successful. You also believe that you have many of the personality characteristics necessary to be outstanding. What should you do next?

You must begin to plan and practice at an early age. Having a mentor or coach to help plan your training and career path is a good way to start. A mentor can provide encouragement and offer constructive criticism of your work.

With the help of a mentor, one of your goals must be to begin developing your talents on a year-round basis. This means practicing almost every day.

To accomplish this, you must learn to listen to the advice and counsel of others. Participation in outside classes or courses may help to raise skill

At 13, Jennifer Capriati was one of the youngest professional tennis players to participate in the sport. Like Chris Evert, she received much support and encouragement from her family.

levels. New ideas and improved techniques can develop better overall skills.

Chris Evert was a world-famous tennis player during the 1970s and '80s. She won many world tennis championships throughout her career.

When Chris was six, her father saw her hitting a tennis ball against a wall. He decided that she should have tennis lessons so that if she did have talent, it would be developed in the proper way. As her interest in tennis increased, her father became her mentor, putting her on a daily training and diet schedule. Working her way through everyday training, she rose to become the second-ranked woman tennis player in the world at the age of fourteen. From there, she went on to fame and fortune in the professional ranks.

Special workshops and summer camps that offer individual training can also increase your skill development. Your own school may offer opportunities for tryouts for teams, plays, and other activities. Participation in these is important, if only for the experience. You may be competing against older or more talented or better coordinated people, but you can learn from the effort even if you do not make the grade. Chalk it up to experience! Next time will be different . . .

Scholarships are available, which also may involve tryouts. A scholarship could provide a free college education if you are talented enough, and college can expose you to higher competitive levels.

Books, magazines, and newspapers are often available on your artistic interest or sport. Reading these can provide useful information or hints to improve your skills. You may also learn how to demonstrate your skills to the right people. Expanding your knowledge about your field can add valuable impetus toward achieving your ultimate goal.

Learning from other people's experience can reduce the mistakes you make. Performers in sports and entertainment fields usually enjoy discussing their experiences. They like to give advice about what they did right and wrong. This could save you valuable time and increase your chances for success.

You will become more self-disciplined from all these activities. By daily practice, you will continually develop the skills you have gained from classes, workshops, tryouts, reading, and interviewing. Always ask yourself: What have I learned? How can it make me an even better performer?

Michael Jordan was a world-class professional basketball player for the Chicago Bulls of the National Basketball Association until his recent retirement.

There are special schools designed to help kids develop their talents. At The Duke Ellington School of the Arts, music and drama students automatically break into singing and acting at the students' first school meeting.

It is not well known that Michael was cut, not once, but twice from his high school basketball team. The frustration seemed to motivate him to work even harder. He dedicated himself to practice, practice, and more practice every day, year-round.

Michael improved at a summer basketball camp, where he learned from others. He was then offered a scholarship to the University of North Carolina, where he became an All-American. Drafted by the

47

You must be able to market your skills if you want to succeed. This young woman is waiting in line to audition for the lead role in the musical *Miss Saigon*. She has brought a photograph of herself to leave with the director so he will remember her easily.

Chicago Bulls, he went on to help the United States win a gold medal in basketball in the 1992 Olympic Games and to become one of the most dominating players in NBA history.

While you are developing your talents, you must also learn about marketing them on a year-round basis. This means informing others what you can do and what experience you have.

Marketing can be a time-consuming task. With 48 the help of a mentor, you may wish to create a skills résumé to keep track of your experiences and successes.

A résumé is a written summary of your career goals, experiences, talents, and education. It can be very helpful in keeping your career focused and headed in the right direction.

As you keep expanding your résumé with new experiences gained, it may make a favorable impression of your accomplishments and may open the door for invitations to specific tryouts. It will show the world that you are organized and dedicated to achieving your goals. Few people are so well organized.

Informing others of your goal and that you are looking for opportunities is called *networking*. It is one of the most successful ways of landing jobs by advertising your talents and skills to the right people.

Questions to Ask Yourself

Both sports and entertainment are extremely competitive fields. If either interests you, it's a good idea to start learning about them now, and get a head start on your career. 1) What opportunities does your school offer that may help you increase your talents and abilities? 2) Whom do you admire most in sports or entertainment? Why? 3) What information about yourself would you include in a résumé?

CHAPTER 5

WHAT HAPPENS IF . . . ?

Working to develop your talents through classes, workshops, tryouts, and so on becomes a difficult task. You must also lead your everyday life—eating, sleeping, going to school, doing homework. Something always seems to interfere with practice.

Your goal is to become the best performer or athlete you can be and make it to the professional ranks. Never lose sight of that if you wish to succeed.

But you may also run into frustrations and setbacks. Expect them, for they will happen. Despite tremendous setbacks, singer Gloria Estefan's drive to continue performing helped her overcome her injuries.

Gloria Estefan is the lead singer and star of the Miami Sound Machine, a popular Latin singing group. She often sings, dances, jumps, and kicks as

Cuban-American singer Gloria Estefan's sky-rocketing career nearly came to an end when her touring bus was hit by a truck in March 1990. Ms. Estefan suffered a broken back. She decided that she wouldn't let her painful injuries keep her from doing what she enjoyed most—performing. Ten months after the accident, she performed live at the Miami Arena.

she performs at concerts. Her Latin-American songs have reached the top of the record charts.

But on March 20, 1990, everything almost came to an end. Her performing travel bus was hit by a truck, and many of the group were hurt. Gloria was seriously injured with a broken back.

After much thought and consultation, she decided that a long and difficult operation was the only way to recover fully. After the surgery, Gloria suffered ex-treme pain. She could sleep less than an hour at a time. **51**

You can join local theater groups to gain experience. These actors belong to the Theatre for the Living City. They perform free at Tompkins Square Park in New York City.

Gloria had worked fourteen years to gain recognition. Now doctors told her it would be three to five years before she could perform again. However, few people realized Gloria's determination to regain what she had lost. She faced her recovery with a positive and determined outlook. Daily exercise increased her strength and physical ability. At the same time, she began to work on her music to help her mental outlook. The road back was tough and difficult.

But less than six months later, Gloria Estefan performed her first concert on the Jerry Lewis Telethon Show. People were amazed at how rapidly **52** *she had recovered. Gloria's determination and posi-*

tive thinking brought her back to where she had been before. She continues to record and to perform throughout the world.

These setbacks may make you think about your goal of being a professional. On one hand, it may stimulate you even more to succeed. On the other hand, you may become discouraged in your attempts.

What happens if you lose interest or realize that you do not have the talent you thought? Then you must face the truth. You must redirect your goals, become flexible in your thinking and attitudes.

This requires great courage. It reveals you as a realistic and down-to-earth person who accepts himself or herself. You may have talents and skills that you can employ in the same field but a related job. In that way you could still be close to the thing you love most.

On the other hand, you may move in a different career direction. If this happens, you must closely review your interests, personality, abilities, and values. Emphasize your strengths. Work on your weaknesses.

Perhaps it might help to talk with a school or career counselor, your parents, or close friends.

Review your past school and work experiences. What has held your interest? What do you really enjoy doing? Try to focus on a *general* career

Whatever direction you pursue, keep in mind that determination usually brings success.

direction. Hold off on a specific choice until you gather more information. Work to learn as much about yourself as possible.

A positive and flexible attitude about yourself and your career goes a long way in helping you find yourself. Things usually happen when you least expect them.

Whatever direction you pursue, continue to be open and enthusiastic toward the future. Most things work out for the best if you see them in a positive light.

Take your time and plan your future carefully. Understanding that circumstances and situations change, usually for the better, will help prepare you for a happy and rewarding career.

Questions to Ask Yourself

Before starting on a career in sports or entertainment, you should think long and hard about whether you think you can really succeed in those fields. 1) What are your goals within the fields of sports or entertainment? 2) Are your goals realistic? 3) What are your strengths and weaknesses with regard to sports or entertainment?

READINESS TEST

At this point in your life, activities in sports or entertainment are enjoyable. You think you might want to make a career as a professional. As we have seen, many factors must be considered before pursuing this goal.

Take this brief paper-and-pencil test. Try to answer as honestly as possible. Score yourself to see if you have what it takes to succeed.

1. Do you believe you have exceptional talent or skill?
   a) Yes. I am a talented and skilled performer. (5 points)
   b) Maybe. Sometimes I think I do. (3 points)
   c) No. I am mostly an average performer. (1 point)
2. Are you able to motivate yourself without encouragement?
   a) Yes. I am highly motivated and consider myself a "self-starter." (5 points)
   b) Sometimes. At times I can be motivated. (3 points)
   c) No. I need others to encourage me. (1 point)
3. Can you take criticism well?
   a) Yes. I can learn from both positive and negative feedback. (5 points)
   b) Sometimes. At times I get angry at negative feedback. (3 points)
   c) No. I often get very angry when others criticize me. (1 point)
4. How do you react to pressure?
   a) Positively. I keep calm and cool under pressure. I thrive on it. (5 points)
   b) Average. Sometimes I react well; other times I don't. (3 points)
   c) Negatively. I work poorly under pressure. (1 point)
5. How competitive are you?
   a) Highly competitive. I always strive to win. (5 points)
   b) At times competitive. I like to compete sometimes. (3 points)

   c) Not very competitive. I just play or perform for fun.
      (1 point)

6. How much patience do you have in achieving goals?
   a) A great deal. I can wait for long periods of time without losing patience. (5 points)
   b) Some. I have some patience with certain things. (3 points)
   c) Little. I want immediate rewards. (1 point)

7. How do you handle frustration?
   a) Well. I take it in stride and vow to do better. (5 points)
   b) Not too well. Sometimes I get angry and pout for a while. (3 points)
   c) Poorly. I react by getting angry and quitting. (1 point)

8. Are you willing to work toward goals that take time?
   a) Yes. I will continually work toward a goal. (5 points)
   b) At times. I get impatient with waiting. (3 points)
   c) No. I want immediate rewards. (1 point)

9. Do you get tired and discouraged easily?
   a) No. I have high energy levels and work toward my goals. (5 points)
   b) Sometimes. I lose energy. (3 points)
   c) Yes. I have low energy to follow through on anything. (1 point)

10. How do you react to failure and defeat?
   a) Well. I do not like losing, but I learn from the experience. (5 points)
   b) Fairly well. I am positive most of the time. (3 points)
   c) Poorly. I react by getting angry and blaming others. (1 point)

Now add up your score and rate yourself as follows:

45–50 pts.   You have *most* of the traits necessary to succeed. Keep up the good work!

35–44 pts.   You have *many* of the traits necessary, but you need to work on some areas.

25–34 pts.   You have a *few* of the traits necessary, but you need to work on many areas.

Below 25   Think about possible "behind the scenes"/"off the field" careers that might be more comfortable for you.

GLOSSARY

agent Person who represents another in settling a sports/entertainment contract.

billing Advertising or promotion of a performance.

bit player One who plays a small role in a show.

booking Scheduling of a group, play, or performance.

call Warning to performers that a show is to begin shortly.

casting Hiring people to play specific roles.

choreography Dance routines in a show.

competitive Having a strong desire to win.

conditioning Training program to improve body performance levels.

contract Legal document describing job performance in exchange for job rewards.

dedication Strong personal desire to complete a goal.

DJ Short for disc jockey.

58 house Slang term for an audience.

instrumentalist Person who plays a musical instrument.

major leagues Highest professional sports level.

manager One who directs or supervises the activities of others.

mentor Person who acts as a coach or adviser.

minor leagues Lower professional sports level.

perseverance Ability to continue pursuit of a goal no matter what the cost.

résumé Summary of a person's goals, education, and job experience.

self-discipline Ability to monitor one's own progress in achieving a goal.

talent Above-average ability.

tryout Attempt to get a part or make a sports team in competition with others.

understudy Back-up person who can replace a performer or athlete in the event of absence or illness.

APPENDIX

Sources of Further Information

Sports Careers

American Alliance for Health, Physical Education and Dance
1900 Association Drive
Reston, VA 22091

Athletic Institute, The
200 Castlewood Drive
North Palm Beach, FL 33408

Major League Baseball Players Association
1370 Avenue of the Americas
New York, NY 10019

National Association of Sports Officials
1700 North Main Street
Racine, WI 53402

National Athletic Trainers Association
P.O. Box 1865
Greenville, NC 27858

National Basketball Players Association
15 Columbus Circle
New York, NY 10023

National Football Players Association
1300 Connecticut Avenue NW
Washington, DC 20036

National Hockey League Players Association
65 Queen Street West
Toronto, Ontario M5H 2M5

Youth Sports, All American
5520 Park Avenue
Trumbull, CT 06611

Entertainment Careers

**American Alliance for Health, Physical
   Education, Recreation and Dance**
1900 Association Drive
Reston, VA 22091

American Dance Guild
31 West 21st Street
New York, NY 10010

American Guild of Musical Artists
1727 Broadway
New York, NY 10105

National Association of Broadcasters
1771 N Street NW
Washington, DC 20036

National Endowment for the Arts
1100 Pennsylvania Avenue NW
Washington, DC 29506

Screen Actors Guild
7065 Hollywood Boulevard
Hollywood, CA 90028

FOR FURTHER READING

Bremmer, Richard. *Michael Jordan—Magic Johnson.* New York: East End Publishing Co., 1989.

Career Discovery Encyclopedia (vols. 1–6). Chicago: J.G. Ferguson Publishing Co., 1990.

Encyclopedia of Careers and Vocational Guidance (vols. 1–4). Chicago: J.G. Ferguson Publishing Co., 1993.

Gonzalez, Fernando. *Gloria Estefan, Cuban-American Singing Star.* Brookfield, CT: Millbrook Press, 1993.

Hopkins, Del and Margaret. *Careers as a Rock Musician.* New York: Rosen Publishing Group, 1993.

Nelson, Cordner. *Careers in Pro Sports.* New York: Rosen Publishing Group, 1992.

Occupational Outlook Handbook (1992–1993). Washington, DC: U.S. Department of Labor, Bureau of Labor Statistics, 1992.

Raber, Thomas. *Joe Montana, Comeback Quarterback.* Minneapolis: Learner Publications, 1989.

Smith, Jay H. *Chris Evert.* Mankato, MN: Creative Education Society, 1975.

Wilson, Beth P. *Stevie Wonder.* New York: G.P. Putnam's Sons, 1979.

INDEX

ABOUT THE AUTHOR

Bruce McGlothlin is a school psychologist/counselor employed by the Allegheny Intermediate Unit in Pittsburgh, Pennsylvania. He holds graduate degrees in both school psychology and counseling. He is the author of several books and games for young adults including *Traveling Light, Great Grooming for Guys, Search and Succeed* and "The Academic/Feeling Trivia Game."

Bruce and his wife, Judi, are the parents of two teenage children, Michael and Molly. Bruce's hobbies are ultramarathon running, biking, snowshoeing, reading, and solving jigsaw puzzles.

COVER PHOTO: © AP/Wide World
PHOTO CREDITS: p. 2 © John Anderson/Impact Visuals; p. 20 © Hazel Hankin/Impact Visuals; p. 32 © Tom McKitterick/Impact Visuals; p. 47 © Shia photo/Impact Visuals; all other photos © AP/Wide World
PHOTO RESEARCH: Vera Ahmadzadeh
DESIGN: Kim Sonsky